Against the Blue

poems by

Julia McConnell

Finishing Line Press
Georgetown, Kentucky

Against the Blue

Copyright © 2016 by Julia McConnell
ISBN 978-1-63534-022-8 First Edition
All rights reserved under International and Pan-American Copyright Conventions.
No part of this book may be reproduced in any manner whatsoever without written permission from the publisher, except in the case of brief quotations embodied in critical articles and reviews.

ACKNOWLEDGMENTS

Thank you to the anthologies where two of these poems first appeared:
A previous version of "Descent" appeared in the anthology *Ain't Nobody That Can Sing Like Me: New Oklahoma Writing*, edited by Jeanetta Calhoun Mish.

"Thanksgiving" originally appeared in the anthology *Oklahoma Poems: And Their Poets*, edited by Nathan Brown.

Gratitude to my writing partner Jeanne Castle and my teachers Jane Vincent Taylor and Anita Skeen. Thank you to my parents for reading poetry to me as a little kid.

Publisher: Leah Maines

Editor: Christen Kincaid

Cover Art: Julia McConnell

Author Photo: Gillian McFall

Cover Design: Elizabeth Maines

Printed in the USA on acid-free paper.
Order online: www.finishinglinepress.com
also available on amazon.com

Author inquiries and mail orders:
Finishing Line Press
P. O. Box 1626
Georgetown, Kentucky 40324
U. S. A.

Table of Contents

That Girl 1
For My First Reader 3
Family Tableau 5
Joint Custody 6
What the Snake Knows 7
My Red Shitkickers 8
ALS Ice Bucket Challenge 9
Visiting Home While in Town for a Conference 11
Evanescence 12
Losing Sight 13
Descent 14
Burial 15
On Buying Rings 16
Thanksgiving 17
Household Agriculture 18
This Is What You've Been Waiting For 19
Driving on highway 17 between Marfa and Ft. Davis 20
Phantom Ring Syndrome 21
This what you gave me 22
Hourglass Half-Full 23
We are all still separate 24
When I think it's over 25

In Memory of Frances Young
1943-2010

That Girl

I unpack the last
ten years of boxes
in reverse:
papers, diplomas,
abandoned projects,
then I come across
the razor blades
and the silver bracelet
cuffs I wore to cover my wounds.

A wailing siren
in my chest
meeting the old lover
the one that drove me crazy
with desire.
That dark eyed woman
of destruction
red dress alluring,
skeletal, burned,
pulling me down
ever deeper
until I wasn't sure
I'd see the surface again.

Bracelets and blades
tarnish and rust.
Silver and steel
should be tossed.

I place them in a tin
and close the lid
wishing I could take
that girl
to get a tetanus shot
if she'd let me,
rub Neosporin into the cuts
bandage the damaged places.
I want to hold her in my arms
tell her *It's all going to be okay*
which wouldn't, exactly,
be lying.

For my first reader

We were in your kitchen
talking while I crushed pills
to mix into your applesauce,
Awkwardly I blurt
For my 30th birthday
I am going to Paris.

I like that better than peyote
or a tattoo. You laughed
from your chair.

A year later I saw
the Eiffel tower, got lost
in the Louvre, ate
Nutella crepes.
I picked out a paving stone
for you from the carriage road
at the Palace of Versailles.

I went to Pere Lachaise
on your death day
to place that stone
on a writer's grave:
Collette, Moliere, Gertrude Stein.

Instead I chose
the most beautiful, most hidden
the private tomb
to place your stone.

Frances, I don't know
how to write a poem for you.

But let me say this:

I continue to place stones for you,
pebbles, ones washed smooth
by the sea, granite, quartz,
slate, jagged rocks that cut
into the palm of my hand.

I am building a monument.

Family Tableau

Because we all want
our sorrow
to be Russian Literature
for Christmas this year
I thought I'd pretend
I was stuck with my family
in a Chekhov play.

But it wasn't
the *Cherry Orchard*
or even *No Exit*.

It was Emily Post
meets *The Simpsons*.
The four of us
trying hard
not to grind our teeth.

On my way out of town
I stopped for gas.
Behind the lamp post
in the parking lot,
over the power plant,
the Arkansas River
and her sandbars,
the sun was setting,
the rose and gold
still holding out
against the blue.

Joint Custody

The door opens. She's standing there
in jeans and a blue t-shirt
I am close enough to admire
her freckles, the straight line of her jaw.
Her hair is cut the way I like it
trimmed close, squaring her face
how it was when we went to Paris.

Our dog is already out the door and dancing
at my feet. She hands me the leash
and looks down at our old puppy
and smiles, pulling back just one corner
of her mouth, not looking at me.

I turn away and walk across the yard
stop and look back. She's watching us go.
I open the car door and the dog jumps in.
I look again. The door is closed.

What the Snake Knows

Why not learn the language of loss?

Shedding is always an itchy process
uncomfortable and unsightly
like all of those old clothes
that don't fit anymore.

Change can be painful as poison
but carrying dead cells
leads to a closet
crammed full of crap.
Unpack those boxes
of disappointment.
Unseal those sacks of guilt.

At times you might feel
your face sloughing off.
Grab that corner
of papery translucence
and pull.

Expose your new skin to the sun.

My Red Shitkickers

Today was a good day
I used to say, pulling
off the boots you bought me,
surprised by my own contentment
after driving through October
fields to Okarche for fried chicken,
or even something as ordinary
as a long and leisurely
trip to Target.

Now I sound like that Patsy Cline
song, *I've got these little things
your work's got you.*
I take my scratched and faded
boots to Ziegler's shoe repair.
They come back with new soles,
the Goodyear tire logo imprinted
on the heels' rubber cap.
I clomp around, heel to toe,
A Good Year,
A Good Year,
A Good Year,
like a prayer,
like an incantation.

ALS Ice Bucket Challenge

Thus shall you think of this fleeting world:
A star at dawn, a bubble in a stream
A flash of lightning in a summer cloud,
A flickering lamp, a phantom, and a dream.
—From the Diamond Sutra

Dear Frances,
This summer all across Facebook
people are dumping buckets of ice
over their heads
in the name of ALS.
From toddlers to celebrities
it's a craze of exuberance
a selfie without context
of a disease
an icy chain letter of swimsuits
and sun in the deadly
heat of August.

It's hard to be jaded
about 94 million dollars
for a disease little known
and less understood.

I wonder what you think.
You just smile and shrug
point me toward stories
of Zen monks taking cold showers
as a path to enlightenment.

I hear us laughing
as we watch folks squealing
and cussing, subjecting themselves
to these chilling showers, defiant,
unwitting, in the face of a disease
that freezes your nerve cells
then your limbs
and, eventually, your lungs.

In video after video I hear
the gasping and sputtering
while buckets of icy impermanence
splash over heads:

Echoes of your last gasps
grief choking me speechless
all of us breathless
with this last lesson
before we die:
Wake Up.

Visiting Home While in Town for a Conference

When I come downstairs
in the early morning
Dad is up and in the kitchen
in a gray sweatshirt and slippers—
the blood thinners give him a chill.

While I sit at the table
and drink my coffee, my dad
toasts the bread he baked
fries an egg in a pan with butter
saying *You like your yolk runny
don't you?* When the egg
is just right he lifts
it from the pan places
it on the toast and sets
the dish before me.

As a little girl eating
breakfast at this same table
I placed all of the cereal
boxes in a square around
my bowl so no one would bother
me while I read the funny papers.

Now Dad sits down to eat
his egg and I jiggle
my crossed legs, nervous
anxious not to be late, yet
wanting to linger, wishing
I had a little more time
to get to know this man.

Evanescence

You smelled like eucalyptus and soap.
You ate veggies in your cereal and swam
laps at the Y on Friday nights.
Peonies thrived in your yard.
Everyone wanted your help.
You loved squares of dark
chocolate and read Rilke
in German to hear it aloud.
One snow day on campus
your husband of 40 years
tackled you playfully to the ground.
As a dancer in college, Martha Graham
once touched you, but you preferred
the Jose Limon technique
of fall and recovery.

This is the hard fall—
only so many of us remember
the music of your silver bangles
falling around your wrists.

Losing Sight

My old dog slowly approaches
her water dish and dips her nose to test
the fullness of the bowl.
I hold a treat against her snout.
She takes it from my hands.
I wonder what it must be like
to feel the world with your face.

She caught her last rabbit in April
when the creature was cornered
in the backyard, too fat
to fit through the chain-link fence.

Now she moves from her blanket
in the bedroom to her pillow
in my office, following
an old path of routine and comfort
bumping into a chair pulled
out from the table or tripping
over a misplaced shoe.

After dinner, I open the back door
to let her out. She walks
like an old lady on ice, gingerly
testing each step before she gives weight.
I walk across the threshold and call
to her, guiding her with my voice
as she steps out into the dark.

Descent

Yesterday cold heavy drops
rained slicking the streets
coating cars, sealing to stone
until all was glazed in ice

transforming my lantern tree
into a Swarovski crystal
bending her branches
outlining her shape
revealing mockingbirds
puffed up against the cold.
Any journey became treacherous.

This morning soft silent
snow descends to the earth.
Wind stirs the limbs
in their glass casings
creaking like weight settling
onto an old leather saddle.

Hypnotized by this downwards
dance I sit in the chill
and squint in the reflected light.

My little tree—
this could be the storm
that will break you
with so much fierce beauty.

Burial

Driving home from the emergency clinic
I make a stop at Ace Hardware.

Our dog is in the backseat
wrapped in blue surgical sheets.

When it was over
they placed her in my arms like a baby

saying, *Her head is here.*
Now standing in front of a wall

of shovels, square and round,
I have to choose:

a tool to plant flowers
or one to scrape ice from stone?

On Buying Rings

I haven't experienced forever
but I know now.
Now becomes now like this ring
all points on it run seamlessly together
requiring calculus to plot such a curve.

I don't know what forever tastes like.
Now tastes like blueberries and ozone
and your skin in the morning.

I can't touch forever
It is an equation in Greek in a textbook
a mirage on the highway
light from a star that has already died.

Now is the word you use to wake
me up in the morning
and when it is time to go to bed.
Now is the word you use to start a game
a bet, a promise.

I want to give you this moment
this particular combination of particles
this mixture of space and time
expanding and contracting
weaving in and out
until I have a whole fabric of time
that I can place around your shoulders.

Thanksgiving

We'd say *Blesses
Owl Lord*
No, that's my Okie.
Try again.

*Blesses Our Lord
And these thine gifts…
Your bounty Christ…*
You are thinking
too hard.
Try again.

*Bless us, Oh Lord
for these thine gifts
which we are about to receive…*
Just Google it.

This prayer I never
thought I would forget.

I wriggled in my chair
when asked to recite
it at dinner.
Felt churning in my stomach
as an altar girl ringing
the bells at consecration.

Now I am trying
to remember
how to say grace.

Household Agriculture

In December you bought me
a glorious poinsettia,
three feet tall in a ten inch pot
wrapped in red foil.

Now it is July and the plant
is a bombed city
bare stems stand
in the rubble of dead leaves.

Sometimes we remember
to water the poor thing
and leave it dripping
in the bathtub overnight,
wondering if it is time
to throw it out.

Half of it lives
and that tender green
leans toward
the window's light.

This is What You've Been Waiting For
    after Marie Howe

For the knowing to enter your body
with what the rumbling
dreams were warning.

After all the sounds
and syllables exchanged,
for your lips to open
into an "o" and close
down on the "ver".
To see her face at the door
watching you drive away.
For the thousand tiny absences,
the granite in your chest.

This is what's been waiting:
Blacktop desert highway
hurtling toward horizon.

Driving on Highway 17 between Marfa and Ft. Davis

After sunset the empty land fills
with black, closes in
so that it's just me
the headlights of my tiny car
three yellow dashes
the occasional flash
of a sign fading into the night.

Even stars are swallowed
by the black.

I want to reach out
switch off the lights
and fly—to disappear
at 90 miles an hour
dissolve into the night
exhilarated, terrified
my foot on the accelerator
pressing into the dark.

Phantom Ring Syndrome

It was a white gold band
channel set with small diamonds.
At first it felt heavy on my hand
and dug into my skin
when I grabbed too hard.
I enjoyed extending
my arm to show it off,
playing at bride.
We didn't plan to marry.

Absence has a shape
and a density.

On the highway after midnight
I tap the fingers of my left hand
against the steering wheel.
Only softness,
where there should be a click,
a tiny impact
of gold and diamonds
between my body
and this vehicle
reckless in the dark.

This is what you gave me

Weekly trips to the city complete
with snacks—oatmeal cookies
and dried apricots. A stack
of empty journals for me to fill
and shipments of books
sent to me in Germany.
Writing dates in the basement
coffee shop at the college library
because you worried about me.

Band aids in a vain attempt
to butterfly a wound. A ride
to the hospital. Walking
by my side into the locked
ward. The next day waiting
in the parking lot to take
me home as I tromped
towards you in flip flops
through the snow.

Or once at the end of a party
I walked up to you dragging
my feet, *Frances,*
I am so tired. Carry me.
And you, no bigger than me
and older than my father,
scooped me up
and held me in your arms.

All we could do
was look at each other
and laugh.

Hourglass Half-Full

I slept past noon this morning.

Actually, it was 11:30.

Last night in a lonesome
haze of red wine
I mistakenly set my alarm
an hour ahead.

I am standing half naked
in my kitchen
staring at my coffee pot
when I realize
every clock in my house is off.

Without asking
she always punched
the right numbers
into all of my clocks.

I grin into my cup
go back to bed
I don't really mind
being out of time.

We are all still separate

Redbuds frozen
in a sudden
spring storm.

Fat toad bleeding
from the lawnmower's lash
jumps into the pond.

Amid hail
and tornado warnings
geese swimming.

Washed up earthworms
struggling on concrete.

Crisp puzzle piece
lost in the grass.

Old dog sitting
in the window
waiting.

Deaf woman lost
she has no way
to get back home.

When I think it's over

I imagine
boxing up books
marking possessions as yours or mine
pulling clothes out of closets
taking pictures off the walls
promising the dogs I'll visit
carrying furniture out the door
until the truck is full
the motor is running
and I'm standing in an empty house
except for a coin
glued to the floor.
I pick at it
until my fingers bleed
and still it won't come loose.
When I walk out
the truck is on fire
and I start running
willing to be burned
wanting to save one last thing.

Julia McConnell is a poet and a librarian in Oklahoma City. She's earned a B.A. in English and a Masters in Library and Information Science from the University of Oklahoma. Julia's work has appeared in *This Land Press, Blood and Thunder, Elegant Rage: A Poetic Tribute to Woody Guthrie, Ain't Nobody That Can Sing Like Me: New Oklahoma Writing,* and *Oklahoma Poems... and Their Poets.* A lifelong Okie, Julia can be seen in her boots stomping through the red dirt with her Jack Russell Terrier, Molly Marlova Magdalena McConnell.

www.ingramcontent.com/pod-product-compliance
Lightning Source LLC
LaVergne TN
LVHW041515070426
835507LV00012B/1579